HEAVENLY

ANGEL

LAY LAY

EXPLAINS WHY

ABORTED BABIES

DO NOT

GO TO HEAVEN

PUBLISHING COMPANY

ISBN: 978-0-6151-7470-9

www.crossover-ministries-publishing.com

TABLE OF CONTENTS

ABORTIONS AND MISCARRIAGES

ABRAHAM AND SARAH

BIBLIOGRAPHY

ABOUT THE AUTHOR

I was dedicated to Jesus Christ of Nazareth as an infant and accepted Him as my Lord and Savior around seven years old when a visiting youth group led me in prayer at the alter. During my Salvation Prayer I asked Jesus to use me in a special ministry. Something that very few other Christians would want to do. I saw all the people just sitting in the pews, the ushers, and the Sunday School teachers and realized any Christian could do that. I wanted something different. One day in church service there was a visiting minister at a church I was visiting as well. The Minister said, "Jesus is going to make you a 'Healer of a Heart'". Then he asked me if I knew what that meant. I said, "No." the minister said, "I don't either, but whatever it is, Jesus is going to use you in a powerful way.

Helping Rachael, Jesus showed me what a 'Healer of the Heart' is. During the course of me helping Rachael to the 'Promised Land', a real Heavenly Angel named Lay Lay and I were allowed one hour one day to talk about Spiritual and Family situations from the King James Version of the Word of God. These books are designed to answer a lot of Spiritual Questions not even your minister can answer or your Church Denomination. I know theology Doctors who can't tell you how people other than Noah and his family made it past the 'Great Flood', yet their names are listed in the King James Version of the Word of God right after the 'World Wide Flood'. These books explain that and much more. I have written these books to tell the whole truth about the Word of God no matter how difficult it may be for me or others. Yes, there are things I write in these books that I don't even like, but in all fairness and total honestly, I must say the WHOLE TRUTH. The title of this book is 100% real. HEAVENLY ANGEL LAY LAY explained to me where aborted babies and babies of miscarriages go and they don't go to Heaven like a lot of people think they do.

INTRODUCTION

The first section of this book tells you where aborted and miscarried babies really go, contrary to popular belief **SPIRITS OF UNBORN BABIES DO NOT GO TO HEAVEN**. The second section of this book contains the good and bad times of Abraham and Sarah as a couple. All scriptures are taken from the King James Version of the Word of God. This book contains an excerpt from my book. MATTHEW'S WORD 'TWO':REAL WORD OF GOD BIBLE.

BOOKS WRITTEN BY WALTER BURCHETT, BA:

MATTHEW'S WORD 'TWO':REAL WORD OF GOD BIBLE   ISBN: 1-4116-6995-9

HEAVENLY ANGEL LAY LAY EXPLAINS WHY ADAM WAS NEVER CURSED
        ISBN: 978-1-84728-176-0

HEAVENLY ANGEL LAY LAY EXPLAINS WHY ABORTED BABIES DO NOT GO TO HEAVEN
        ISBN: 978-0-6151-7470-9

HEAVENLY ANGEL LAY LAY EXPLAINS THE BIBLICAL GROUNDS FOR MARRIAGE,
        SEPARATION, AND DIVORCE   ISBN: 978-0-6151-7481-5

HEAVENLY ANGEL LAY LAY EXPLAINS WHY PROFESSIONAL COUNSELORS HAVE 'HARDENED
        HEARTS'   ISBN: 978-0-6151-7482-2

HEAVENLY ANGEL LAY LAY EXPLAINS THE DIFFERENCE BETWEEN A 'COLD CHRISTIAN' AND
        A 'BACKSLIDER'   ISBN: 978-0-6151-7483-9

HEAVENLY ANGEL LAY LAY EXPLAINS WHICH BIBLE TO READ, WHICH BIBLE NOT TO READ,
        AND WHY   ISBN: 978-0-6151-7484-6

HEAVENLY ANGEL LAY LAY EXPLAINS WHY GAYS, LESBIANS, BI-SEXUALS, AND
        TRANSSEXUALS DO NOT GO TO HEAVEN   ISBN: 978-0-6151-7485-3

HEAVENLY ANGEL LAY LAY EXPLAINS WHY CHILDREN AND SPORTS ARE DEFINITELY A
        RELIGION IN TODAY'S SOCIETY   ISBN: 978-0-6151-7486-0

HEAVENLY ANGEL LAY LAY EXPLAINS WHAT 'MANY ARE CALLED, BUT FEW ARE CHOSEN
        REALLY MEANS   ISBN: 978-0-6151-7487-7

HEAVENLY ANGEL LAY LAY AND GUARDIAN ANGEL SHADOW GUESS THE REAL AGE OF THE
        EARTH   ISBN: 978-0-6151-7488-4

AN ABUSED MAN'S BATTLES, TRYING TO PROTECT HIS BOYS   ISBN: 978-0-6151-5191-5

HEAVENLY

ANGEL

LAY LAY

EXPLAINS WHY

ABORTED BABIES

DO NOT

GO TO HEAVEN

The following is an excerpt from my book called, **MATTHEW'S WORD 'TWO':REAL WORD OF GOD BIBLE**. This is one of the Bible Mysteries Heavenly Angel Lay Lay shared with me on our way, taking Rachael to the Promised Land. Since a Heavenly Angel told me this, how can I change anything that any Heavenly Angel said and make it better? If you don't know who Heavenly Angel Lay Lay is or how I was allowed to work with three different Heavenly Angels, then you will need to purchase **MATTHEW'S WORD 'TWO':REAL WORD OF GOD BIBLE** and read it (ISBN: 1-4116-6995-9). The first half of **MATTHEW'S WORD 'TWO':REAL WORD OF GOD BIBLE** is about how I was allowed to work with three different Heavenly Angels to begin with. The second half of **MATTHEW'S WORD 'TWO':REAL WORD OF GOD BIBLE** contains about 100 pages of Biblical facts Heavenly Angel Lay Lay was allowed to share with me. You will need to read the whole book in order to understand how I was allowed to work with three different Heavenly Angels for a little over a year of my life. Lay Lay explained to me why Adam didn't stop Eve from eating the 'forbidden fruit', what caused Cain to get so angry he killed Abel, what happened to the Raven from Noah's Ark and why it had to be the Raven that was let out first and then the Dove, how old the Earth really is, along with other Biblical Secrets that theologians and theorists do not know.

THE 'GREAT GULF': ABORTIONS AND MISCARRIAGES

(Heavenly Angel Lay Lay and I are talking at this point about different subjects in the King James Version of the Word of God)

I asked, "Speaking of human souls, when does the soul and spirit go into the human?" Lay Lay said, "At the same time the sperm goes into the egg, and the same time the sex of the human is spiritually created. It's all done in the 'twinkling of an eye'. There are several different stages of growth to a human in and out of the mother's womb. Just because humans can't see the stages doesn't mean the stages don't exist. Even today, scientists can't explain how the human mind works, but it works just the same. That's why the girls thought Damien was a 'clone'; they couldn't detect a soul in the vessel with their powers. A clone won't have a human soul or spirit.

In Job 3:10-26 (KJV)
10) Because it shut not up the doors of my mother's womb, nor hid sorrow from mine eyes.
11) Why died I not from the womb? why did I not give up the ghost when I came out of the belly?
12) Why did the knees prevent me? or why the breasts that I should suck?
13) For now should I have lain still and been quiet, I should have slept: then had I been at rest,
14) With kings and counsellors of the earth, which build desolate places for themselves;
15) Or with princes that had gold, who filled their houses with silver:
16) Or as an hidden untimely birth I had not been; as **INFANTS WHICH NEVER SAW LIGHT.**
17) There the wicked cease from troubling; and there the weary be at rest.
18) There the prisoners rest together, they hear not

the voice of the oppressor.
19) The small and great are there; and the servant
is free from his master.
20) Wherefore is light given to him that is in
misery, and life unto the bitter in **soul**;
21) Which long for death, but it cometh not; and
dig for it more than for hid treasures;
22) Which rejoice exceedingly, and are glad, when
they can find the grave?"

I asked, "Why are there so many birth
defects and things?" Lay Lay said, "Some of it's
due to the mother's usage to 'the pill' and other
medication, drinking and drugs. Some is due to
the sins of the father or mother or others in the
family tree before them. The three to four
generation curse has some to do with it. Rachael
and Damien both are products of the three to four
generation curse. They are both the fourth
generation of the four generation curse, but with
Jesus there is a way out. The first thing that
happens is Jesus sees the faith of the humans not
only who are cursed, but those who are praying
with the human who is cursed as well. Then Jesus
forgives the human for the sins in the Physical
Bloodline, and creates the Spiritual Bloodline just
like you did. You were praying for Detta from
your heart when you told Jesus to go ahead and
sanctify Detta through you. You broke the
Physical Bloodline through the 'sanctification'
through you to Jesus Christ of Nazareth. Then
Jesus heals the human as well as forgiving them of
the sins of their ancestors and theirs as well. Now
Jesus can protect Detta even though she hasn't
Crossed Over yet. Jesus is still allowed to protect
her as His own child because of you. Jesus just
made it so His children wouldn't have to suffer

three to four generations. Before, there was no way around the generational curse, now there is." I asked, "What is the purpose of the 'three to four generation curse'? I mean, I can understand God doing something to the two who committed the sin, but why curse the children to the fourth generation?" Lay Lay said, "Actually they are getting off easy. Look what happened to Adam and Eve when they 'ate of the fruit', all mankind was cursed then. The Israelites were used to the customs of Egypt. Just like Detta is used to the customs of the Satanists. It takes time for those customs to be broken, and God did give them time. Then He put His foot down and said 'NO MORE'. The Israelites continued with the customs, so He cursed the offspring for the ones who actually committed the abomination to see, as a reminder of what would happen if the custom was continued. Every time the ones who committed the abomination saw their children, grandchildren, great grandchildren, then were reminded of their terrible act they were told by God not to do. Their offspring was a constant reminder of the new laws of God. You also have to remember, back then people lived for hundreds of years. So the ones who did the abomination was literally reminded for all those centuries what they did. Now humans don't live as long and Jesus made a way out of that curse for each human on an individual basis." (Jesus made sure I knew Tony and Rachael are 1st Cousins, Damien and Gabriella are 2nd cousins. Tony and Rachael were married in the Village and had two legitimate girls, those girls are in Heaven now because they died before the 'age of accountability'. Damien and Gabriella had to get married for their babies to be considered 'Legitimate' in the 'Proper Physical

Bloodline'. In order for their children to be in the Proper Physical Bloodline the couples weren't allowed to be committing an abomination. When Detta was being 'corrected' married to Tony, the men were allowed to torture Detta with foreign objects, and Tony was allowed to hold her hand during that time, but the men were not allowed to have sex with Detta because that would have caused doubt about who the father of the two girls really were. There could be no doubt about the 'legitimacy' of their baby girls. That's the reason for the 'trial marriage' in the Satanist Village to begin with, to get Tony and Rachael as Husband and Wife, even if they didn't know it. Even Satanists have to be married for the babies to be considered 'legitimate' and in the 'Proper Physical Bloodline' and not 'bastards' or 'bitches'.)

I asked, "What about 'spare the rod, and spoil the child'?" Lay Lay said, "God always warns His children before He does anything drastic. Most of the time, He warned them a few times. Then if they didn't pay any attention or forgot and went right back worshipping the Idols again, He was drastic. Yes, you need to spank children, or slap them every once in a while. It's like a 'wake-up call' to the children. Children will push a parent or any adult to see how far the child can get before the adult gets on their case. That's how they learn their boundary lines. Once the adult does spank them or slap them a few times, the child usually knows pretty much what is expected of the child, then the child will obey the adult. If the mother or child runs to the police or social services every time something like that happens, the mother is proving to the child that the child doesn't have to mind the boyfriend, father, or husband which defeats the purpose of the discipline to begin with and causes havoc in the family. The family unit isn't living by the Real Word of God. That's one big reason juvenile halls, jails, and prisons are full today. Yes, children need spanked or slapped every once in a while to keep them in the boundary lines. Jesus spanks all His children on occasion. If you don't spank the child at times, you will spoil them or if you call legal help that spoils them as well. Then the child will know they can do anything and get away with it. Just like the Preacher's Kid that Detta punched out at Camp Meeting. Jesus knew he was getting too smart for his own good, and the parents weren't doing anything about it so Jesus allowed Detta to smack him a good one, literally knocking him out. If Jesus wouldn't have allowed Detta to knock him out, he would have kept fighting round after round and not thought anything of it. Jesus wanted him to feel the pain and teach him a lesson. The boy was picking on Detta and thinking he was better than her. A Christian isn't any better than anyone else. Just like you when you and Damien talked, you know in your heart Damien isn't any better than you are. You just have more power in you, but you don't boast about it unless you have to get your point across to someone like Damien. After you faced Damien head-on, Damien had respect for you. Once you found out the whole truth about what was going on and Damien wanting to help the girls, you had respect for Damien as well, even though you are a Christian and he is a Satanist. That knock-out brought the boy back into the boundary lines of what Jesus set for him. As Shadow and I said before, 'It's good to fight at times, it releases tension between two or more people. The tension isn't bottled up and therefore the positive emotions can flow through the vessel again', that's the way humans are made. As far as the man and woman fighting, they may need to every once in a while as well. A lot of that depends on their background, family interference, and their maturity." I said, "A lot of counselors think there are other solutions around that." Lay Lay said, "The only other solution around that is when the vessel dies and goes to Heaven. What counselors want on Earth will NEVER happen as long as Satan is 'roaming to and fro'. Nothing will take the place of a good spanking when the child needs it. That extra padding on the rump isn't there just to sit down on, it's there for protection of the bone when the rod is smacking the rumpus as well." I asked, "Would a 'foreign object' be considered a weapon if it's used for spanking?" Lay Lay said, "'The 'Rod' is a 'foreign object'. It is still used to spank children in some countries. The 'Rod' actually does it's intended purpose. Just because the parents use a 'foreign object' on their children's butts to get the children's attention and not allow them to stray from the truth instead of their hand doesn't mean the parent did anything wrong. Just like Detta hit the boy with her closed fist right on the jaw. Jesus knew exactly what would happen before it happened. Jesus knew that boy was going to get hit in the jaw by Detta and He allowed it. Detta didn't hit that boy on his butt. In the same sense, it was just enough to do the intended job, just like you did with Damien. Like you told DJ, only use as much force as necessary to protect yourself. Just because a man has the power and authority over his wife and children doesn't mean the man has to use the power to the extreme. Jesus only uses as much force as necessary to get the job done."

ABRAHAM

AND

SARAH

(CONTINUED FROM: ABRAM AND SARAI IN MY BOOK HEAVENLY ANGEL LAY LAY EXPLAINS WHY ADAM WAS NEVER CURSED)

After I tell the reader Biblical Facts that Heavenly Angel Lay Lay told me when I was working with her and Shadow, I will be writing about different stories from the King James Version of the Word of God talking about the family aspects in the Word of God. How the different couples in the bible met, what the couples went through, and what men, women, and children are commanded to do and not to do according to the Word of God. Just like HEAVENLY ANGEL LAY LAY taught me how to do.

ABRAHAM AND SARAH

Abraham and Sarah are in Kadesh-Barnea and Hagar is pregnant with Abraham's baby.

Genesis 16:1-16

1) Now <u>Sarai Abram's wife</u> bare him no children: and she had an handmaid, an Egyptian (the Pharaoh's daughter), whose name *was* Hagar. [God already told Abram the servant from Damascus was not to be his heir and Sarai knew this. Why would God want a servant from Egypt to be Abram's heir? God wouldn't. God didn't want Abram's heir to come from anyone other than Abram and Sarai. God had already promised Abram that his and Sarai's children would inherit all the blessings of God and Abram and Sarai's children would be too numerous to number, remember? It wasn't God's appointed time yet, and Sarai leaned on her own understanding instead of what God had told Abram. In today's terms, Sarai got tired of waiting on God and started thinking about other ways to have children, which opened the door for Satan to get Sarai to think Abram was to pregnant Hagar (Satan's child), a handmaid with an Egyptian background,

instead of Sarai to have a child]

2) And Sarai said unto Abram, Behold now, the LORD hath restrained me from bearing: I pray thee, go in unto my maid; **it may be** (you notice these words? Sarai, herself, isn't even sure, there is doubt and confusion) **that I may obtain children by her** (Now this is Sarai talking, leaning on her own understanding. Back then the custom was if the maid delivers the child of the master then the child is considered a child of the master and his wife. Sarai was leaning on her own understanding and going by the culture of their land at that time, allowing her emotions to think for her instead of trusting God. There's that short-term thinking of a woman, not being able to think long-term and the effects of the decision. The difference between Adam and Eve and Abram and Sarai is that Adam didn't know anything about eating the 'forbidden fruit' until he had already eaten a bite of the apple where Abram took a part in the process. Adam and Eve is fully explained by Heavenly Angel Lay Lay in my books MATTHEW'S WORD 'TWO':REAL WORD OF GOD BIBLE and in HEAVENLY ANGEL LAY LAY EXPLAINS WHY ADAM WAS NEVER CURSED). And Abram hearkened (Listened) to the voice (Influential power) of Sarai.

3) And Sarai Abram's wife took Hagar her maid the Egyptian, **after Abram had dwelt ten years in the land of Canaan** (this is an important fact to know. Abram and Sarai had tried to conceive a child for **TEN YEARS** and was still unsuccessful before Sarai said, 'Take Hagar and get her pregnant, we will have a child by her'. Abram was 85 and Sarai was 75 now. Again, this sound like a modern day 'surrogate mother'. The man gets another woman pregnant because the man's wife can't conceive and the child is supposed to go to the man and his wife. Then just before the delivery the woman who is actually carrying the baby changes her mind and there are a lot of court room battles over visitation when the other father and mother wants to have a say in how the child is raised. The only ones who win those battles are the attorneys and counselors with all their 'high fees'. Of course if no one has any money, the attorneys and counselors aren't interested in representing the parties involved), and gave her (Hagar) to her (Sarai's) husband Abram **to be his, (Abram's) wife** (Even laying, having sex with a servant makes the

servant the wife of the master according to the custom of the land, then Hagar is Abram's wife as well as Sarai, but the custom of the land doesn't change the Word of the Living God, or excuse any sin and what Sarai allowed Abram to do with Hagar. How was it a sin? Sarai **nagged** Abram long enough that Abram went against what God said, Sarai was 'not in submission' to Abram as God had commanded for all women to be to their husbands. Just like Heavenly Angel Lay Lay said in 'MATTHEW'S WORD 'TWO':REAL WORD OF GOD BIBLE. Just like today in the United States, if the man doesn't do what the woman wants, and he raises his voice to her, she could have him removed from the property with a 'restraining order' saying 'he scared me, I'm afraid of him'. Wow, if Abram had been served like that, we would still be sacrificing lambs for our sins. A lot of people talk about the Twelve Tribes of Israel, which is the sons of Jacob, but Jacob is one of the Ten Tribes of Abraham. If Abram and Sarai had been separated by a 'Restraining Order' for a full year like women do today, then the Twelve Tribes of Israel would never have been born. Sarai not only allows Abram to get Hagar pregnant with Abram's sperm, but Sarai insists on it. Yes, a custom of their land at that time, but still not what God had said to Abram and Abram told Sarai what God had said, that's why Abram and Sarai kept trying for **TEN YEARS** to begin with. Abram and Sarai left Haran and came into Canaan ten years ago. God didn't tell Abram to take Hagar in and get her pregnant, Sarai leaned on her own understanding and a woman's short-term thinking, not what God had said to Abram. Abram listened to Sarai's 'influential power'. Both Adam and Abraham listened to their wives influential power and their wives turned out to be wrong and both wives also turned out to regret what they influenced their husbands to do. The only difference between Abram and Adam is <u>Abram knowingly took part</u> in the process where <u>Adam didn't know anything about eating the 'forbidden fruit' until he had already eaten of it</u>. That's at the beginning of this book)

4) And he (Abram) went in unto Hagar, (If you think Abram didn't lay with Hagar several times in that respect you're kidding yourself. He laid with Hagar several times, until everyone knew Hagar had conceived Abraham's child. Remember what Heavenly Angel Lay Lay said about comma's and semi-colons in the Word of God? There

is a comma after Hagar, meaning it took a while for Hagar to conceive. Abram and Hagar continued having sex with each other, day and night into weeks and possibly even months until Hagar didn't have her period when she was supposed to. If you think Abram and Hagar didn't develop feelings for each other during that period of time, you're kidding yourself again. How many women today try to get pregnant and don't get pregnant on the first try naturally. It may take months for a woman to intentionally become pregnant. Remember, God wasn't in this pregnancy, Abram, Sarai, and Hagar were doing this on their own) and she (Hagar) conceived: (Now the semi-colon) and when she (Hagar) saw that she (Hagar) had conceived, her (Hagar's) mistress (Sarai) was despised in her (Hagar's) eyes (Hagar felt 'equal' to Sarai once Hagar felt Abram's sperm hitting her vaginal walls the first time, that made Hagar 'equal' to Sarai. There was nothing physically that Hagar hadn't had from Abram that Sarai didn't have. After a while there was nothing emotionally Hagar hadn't felt from Abram as well. They had developed feelings for each other. Then when Hagar had conceived from Abram's sperm, Hagar had something, or in this case someone inside her from Abram that Sarai never had, Abram's child, which made Hagar feel 'above' Sarai. Reminds me of men and women today having affairs and the married person's lover feeling not only equal to the lovers' spouse, but better than the lovers' spouse because now, the lover feels the married person wants the lover more than the married person wants their own spouse, which in some cases is actually true. That's why Lay Lay talked about 'Phone Sex' and 'Cyber Sex' and the effects they have on married couples as well. Or the 'surrogate mother' wants the man whose sperm impregnated the 'surrogate mother' when the man's wife couldn't, or their own husband because now the two of them are sharing something special together, a child. Then you have spouses fighting each other, laying the blame on each other and court battles over visitation rights and the rearing of the child, not to mention the child support the 'would have been surrogate mother', now wanting to be the 'natural mother and legal and physical mother' of the child wants from the natural father now that the 'would have been 'surrogate mother' wants to keep the baby after the baby is born. Satan sure does make a lot of heart ache when we step out of God's will for our lives and rely on our own understanding)

5) And **Sarai said** unto Abram, **My wrong** *be* upon thee (Sarai realizes she did the wrong thing after it was too late. Reminds me of Eve realizing she did the wrong thing by listening to the serpent after it was too late and a lot of women today after their emotions settle down knowing in their hearts they did the wrong thing after it's too late): I have given my maid into thy (your) bosom (Abram's private part and emotions to go along with it. Abram and Hagar developed feelings for each other); and when she (Hagar) saw that she had conceived, I was despised in her eyes: the LORD judge between me and thee (This sounds like the husband and wife arguing over another man or woman. Now Sarai is trying to lay the blame on Abram when Sarai, herself not only gave Abram permission to have sex with Hagar several times, but actually insisted on Abram culturally marrying Hagar. Reminds me of women today having an idea, telling their man and when their man does as the woman asks and the idea doesn't turn out the way the woman expected, the woman blames the man. Then on the other hand, the woman nags the man until he gives her what she wants even though he knows it shouldn't be done, then after the woman sees it was a mistake, blames the man anyway).

6) But Abram said unto Sarai, Behold, thy maid *is* in thy hand (Abram is telling Sarai, 'It was your idea, you deal with it'); do to her as it pleaseth thee. And when Sarai dealt hardly with her (Hagar), she (Hagar) fled from her (Sarai's) face." (I know Sarai didn't kick Hagar out here, but who wants to stick around after someone tells you to do something and then after the fact, get punished for doing what you are told to do?)

7) And the angel of the LORD found her (Hager) by a fountain of water in the wilderness, by the fountain in the way to Shur.

8) And he said, Hagar, Sarai's maid, whence camest thou? And whither wilt thou go? And she said, I flee from the face of my mistress Sarai.

9) And the angel of the LORD said unto her (Hagar), Return to thy (your) mistress, and submit thyself (yourself) under her (Sarai's) hands.

10) And the angel of the LORD said unto her (Hagar) I will multiply

thy (your) seed (offspring) exceedingly, that it (The number of offspring) shall not be numbered for multitude.

11) And the angel of the LORD said unto her (Hagar), Behold, thou *art* with child, and shalt bear a son, and shalt call his name Ishmael; because the LORD hath heard thy (your) affliction.

12) And he (Ishmael) will be **a wild man**. (How did God know Ishmael would be a 'wild man', 'possessed'? God knew Hagar was not His child and she would choose an Egyptian wife for Ishmael that worshipped 'idols' and 'false gods'. Abram and Sarai put hatred in Hagar's heart after the way they treated her and Ishmael. Remember, demons can possess animate and inanimate objects, meaning statues, pictures, children's play toys on the market today, etc., and anything that is living as well. There is a whole section about this in my book MATTHEW'S WORD 'TWO':REAL WORD OF GOD BIBLE explaining demonic possession and animate (living) and inanimate (non-living) objects (For everyone who doesn't know what 'animate' and 'inanimate' meant, don't worry. I didn't either when Heavenly Angel Lay Lay used those terms on me, I had to ask her what they meant). Worshipping false gods would make Ishmael 'demonically possessed' just like the man with the Legion of demons in him when Jesus sent the legion into the herd of swine. Remember, his being possessed made him a 'wild man'. There were also a few other people in the New Testament that Christ and the Apostles dealt with and delivered); his hand *will be* against every man (He will fight against every man), and every man's hand against him (Every man will fight against him. The results of being possessed by this certain type of demon.); and he shall dwell in the presence of all his brethren (A vessel can be possessed by many more than just one unclean spirit. Remember what Lay Lay said about how many demons are a legion? She said, 'Two or more depending on the type and strength of each demon.' The first was making Ishmael a 'wild man'. Just like the little boy who was playing with all the children's play toys resembling children's cartoon characters on television when the character gets their super powers from outside sources. It's really Friendly Unclean Spirits and Regular Unclean Spirits playing around allowing the Friendly Unclean Spirits win all the time to get the parents to buy the toys for the children, thinking the children are

learning right from wrong. Jesus, Himself, said, 'It's only a matter of time before the boy is possessed with an Unclean Spirit anyway. The boy is playing with toys who get their powers from outside power sources.' Those toys, like statues, or pictures are 'inanimate objects' and can be possessed by 'unclean spirits' who transfer into humans, including children. There is a whole section in my book MATTHEW'S WORD 'TWO':REAL WORD OF GOD BIBLE talking about children's toys. Remember what Heavenly Angel Lay Lay said, 'Look at the characteristics, not the titles').

13) And she (Hagar) called the name of the LORD that spake (spoke) unto her (Hagar), Thou (your) God seest (sees) me (Hagar): for she (Hagar) said, Have I also here looked after him that seeth me?

14) Wherefore the well was called **Beerlahairoi**; behold, *it is* between **Kadesh and Bered**.

15) And Hagar bare Abram a son: and Abram called his son's name, which Hagar bare, Ishmael.

16) And **Abram was fourscore and six years old (86 years old), when Hagar bare Ishmael to Abram**. (Now we know that Abram committed adultery several times with Hagar at the request of Sarai. This reminds me of a few private organizations that the man is allowed to take another man's wife into the bedroom as long as that man is on a certain list of close friends of the man who is married to the woman being taken into the bedroom and make love to the woman whenever he wants in order for the newcomer to become a member of that particular organization. This is not 'hearsay', I have seen this happen with my own two eyes with a girl I used to go to high school with. Not only do I know this woman, I knew her parents before they died. There were three men who had sex with her that night and her husband was right there while they were putting their hands all over her body and kissing her and he allowed it. After that these men were allowed to come in and take her into the bedroom any time the men wanted to have sex with her. It was the man and woman's initiation into this particular private organization. A well known organization that everyone has heard about. Remember, I lived in Stanfield, Oregon at that time, it's a small town, not a big city. If you think things like that don't happen in small towns, think again. Up to this point Abram and Sarai are still together traveling a lot. Abram and

Sarai are still in Kadesh-Barnea)

Genesis 17:1-27

1) And when **Abram was ninety years old and nine**, the LORD appeared to Abram, and said unto him, I am the Almighty God; walk before me, and be thou perfect. (This was 13 years after Ishmael was born.)

2) And I will make my covenant between me and thee, and will multiply thee exceedingly.

3) And Abram fell on his face: and God talked with him, saying,

4) As for me, behold, my covenant is with thee, and thou shalt be a father of many nations.

5) Neither shall thy name any more be called Abram, but thy name shall be Abraham; for a father of many nations **have I made thee**. (We need to pay attention to something here. God is using the 'past tense' even though nothing has happened yet)

6) And I will make thee exceeding fruitful, and I will make nations of thee, and kings shall come out of thee.

7) And I will establish my covenant between me and thee and thy seed after thee in their generations for an everlasting covenant, to be a God unto thee, and to thy seed after thee.

8) And I will give unto thee, and to thy seed after thee, the land wherein thou art a stranger, all the land of Canaan, for an everlasting possession (here is God's promise to the Israelites); and I will be their God (Here is the stipulation that the Israelites need to keep with God in order to keep God's promise to them).

9) And God said unto Abraham, Thou shalt keep my covenant therefore, thou, **and thy seed after thee in their generations** (the problem is that the Israelites never kept their part of the covenant just like Heavenly Angel Lay Lay said. The Israelites still have the land because of God's promise to Abraham and the 'Proper Physical Bloodline', but their Birthright to Heaven is now on an individual bases as other scriptures in the Old Testament indicate when God divorced the Nation of Israel and will now judge each person on an individual bases, the 'Spiritual Bloodline').

10) This is my covenant, which ye shall keep, between me and you and thy seed after thee; Every man child among you shall be

circumcised.

11) And ye shall circumcise the flesh of your foreskin; and it shall be a token of the covenant betwixt (between) me and you.

12) And he that is eight days old shall be circumcised among you, every man child in your generations, he that is born in the house, or bought with money of any stranger, which is not of thy seed.

13) He that is born in thy house, and he that is bought with thy money, must needs be circumcised: and **my covenant shall be in your FLESH for an everlasting covenant** (This is why the Israelites still have the land, the land is of the flesh, but the family of God is in the Spiritual World and they are no longer His chosen people as a nation, but now the Israelites just like everyone, else is judged on an individual basis).

14) And the uncircumcised man child whose flesh of his foreskin is not circumcised, that soul shall be cut off from his people; he hath broken my covenant.

15) And God said unto Abraham, As for Sarai thy wife, thou shalt not call her name Sarai, but Sarah shall her name be.

16) And I will bless her, and give thee a son also of her: yea, I will bless her, and she shall be a mother of nations; kings of people shall be of her.

17) Then <u>Abraham</u> fell upon his face, and laughed, and said in his heart, Shall a child be born unto him that <u>is an hundred years old</u>? and shall <u>Sarah, that is ninety years old</u>, bear?

18) And Abraham said unto God, O that Ishmael might live before thee! (Even though Abraham was begging God to use Ishmael for the inheritance, God knew it was not possible. The heir of Abraham and the nations had to come from BOTH parents of the 'Proper Physical Bloodline, not just one)

19) And God said, **Sarah thy wife shall bear thee a son indeed** (God is reinforcing what He said earlier); and thou shalt call his name Isaac: and I will establish my covenant with him for an everlasting covenant, *and* with his seed after him (Every covenant has two sides, one from God and one from the human God makes the covenant with).

20) And as for Ishmael, I have heard thee: Behold, I have blessed him, and will make him fruitful, and will multiply him exceedingly;

twelve <u>princes</u> shall he beget, and I will make him a great nation. [Now if any of you fathers or mothers out there who are out of marital wedlock with 'bastards' or 'bitches' think your child is the same as a child born in wedlock, you are wrong, nothing can change that fact. The Blood of Christ can change your 'bastard' or 'bitch' to the 'Spiritual Bloodline' from the 'Physical Bloodline', but they can never be changed to the 'Proper Physical Bloodline'. That's why Damien and Gabriella had to be married before the babies were born so the babies would be in the 'Proper Physical Bloodline'. Satan can't change that because God won't allow that to be changed. Jesus, Himself, can't even change that, those are the rules in the Spiritual World and we are always in the Spiritual World whether we can physically see the Spiritual World or not. Lay Lay went into great detail about the difference between the 'Spiritual Bloodline, Proper Physical Bloodline, and Physical Bloodline' in MATTHEW'S WORD 'TWO':REAL WORD OF GOD BIBLE. God promised Abraham that Abraham's seed (offspring) would be blessed].

21) **But my covenant will I establish with ISAAC, which SARAH SHALL BEAR UNTO THEE AT THIS SET TIME IN THE NEXT YEAR.** [Ishmael never did get a covenant with God like Isaac did. When we are ready to move up in His Work, God gives us more, better jobs to do. God even gave Abraham and Sarah up to a year to prepare for the upcoming delivery. 'BEAR and <u>IN THE NEXT YEAR</u>' doesn't really specify it was a whole year, it may have just been a part of a year, like nine months. Sarah may have been pregnant at this time. As many Christians as I have talked to pertaining to God doing something special in their lives, they all said the same thing. They didn't really understand what was going to happen, but God was preparing them (The Holy Spirit Preparing the Way again) for something special to happen. Then at the last minute (or so they thought), all the doors opened and their blessing flowed from Heaven. Whether it was for them to move to a better position at work, get a raise, see relatives, or actually move to a different location. See, when a Christian GROWS IN HIM, He does move us around according to our growth. We think it's at the last minute that He intervenes, but in all actuality, it's not, it just takes us that much time to grow in Him enough for Him to be able to move us up in His

work. He made us a promise not to give us more than we can handle and if a Christian isn't ready to handle anymore, then He won't put us in that higher position. He will wait until we are rested or learned in His Word enough and then help us get on our way again. It just seems to us that He waits until the last minute because He moves at the end of our rest or learning period. Like these books that I write now. I needed about five years to rest between the time I helped Rachael because I was dealing with the Supernatural a lot, 1998-2000, and the time I started writing the book about helping her, 2005 and published in 2006. Now by the time 2007 comes along I will have several books written, but also be ready to settle down with an overseas wife and have a family as Heavenly Angel Lay Lay said I would. Five years ago I wasn't even considering someone from overseas. Being all rested after the battles with Satan and the Spiritual World that I went through, I'm ready to have a girlfriend, get to know her, and let the Holy Spirit Prepare us for each other. Rachael and I encountered several Spiritual things, some I had time to ask Heavenly Angel Lay Lay about and others I didn't]

22) And he (God) left off talking with him (Abraham), and God went up from Abraham.

23) And Abraham took Ishmael his son, and all that were born in his house, and all that were bought with his money, every male among the men of Abraham's house; and circumcised the flesh of their foreskin in the selfsame day, as God had said unto him.

24) And **Abraham was** ninety years old and nine **(99 years old)**, when he was circumcised in the flesh of his foreskin.

25) And **Ishmael his son was thirteen years old**, when he was circumcised in the flesh of his foreskin.

26) In the selfsame day was Abraham circumcised, and Ishmael his son.

27) And all the men of his house, born in the house, and bought with money of the stranger, were circumcised with him.

Genesis 18:1-17, 33

1) And **the LORD appeared** unto him (Abraham) in the plains of Mamre (still living in Hebron): and he sat in the tent door in the heat of the day;

2) And he lift up his eyes and looked, and, lo, (look) three men stood by him: and when he saw them, he ran to meet them from the tent door, and bowed himself toward the ground (Two angels and God Himself, I know some say three angels, but look again at verse one. It says, 'the LORD appeared'),

3) And said, <u>My LORD,</u> if now I have found favour in thy sight, pass not away, I pray thee, from thy servant: (Abraham recognized Him as being the LORD Himself)

4) Let a little water, I pray you, be fetched, <u>and wash your feet, and rest yourselves under the tree</u>: (God and angels in human form)

5) And <u>I will fetch a morsel of bread,</u> and comfort ye your hearts; after that ye shall pass on: for therefore are ye come to your servant. And they said, **So do, as thou hast said**. (Talking just like angels, short and to the point. They understand the 'power of the tongue' and 'speaking things into existence')

6) And <u>Abraham hastened into the tent unto Sarah,</u> and said, Make ready quickly three measures of fine meal, knead it, and make cakes upon the hearth. (God can eat food in human form and angels eat food also. Remember 'Shadow', Rachael's 'Protecting Angel' when Shadow was talking to the demon? Shadow said, 'No thanks, I enjoy my steak every night too much.' That whole incident is in MATTHEW'S WORD 'TWO':REAL WORD OF GOD BIBLE)

7) And Abraham ran unto the herd, and fetcht a calf tender and good, and gave it unto a young man; and he hasted to dress it.

8) And he (Abraham) took butter, and milk, and the calf which he had dressed, and set it before them; and he stood by them under the tree, and they did eat.

9) And they (God and the two angels) said unto him (Abraham), Where is Sarah thy wife? And he (Abraham) said, Behold, in the tent.

10) And he (God) said, I will certainly return unto thee (you) according to the time of life; and, lo, Sarah thy wife shall have a son. And Sarah **heard it in the tent** door, which was behind him. (Sarah was in the tent. Sarah never saw God or the angels. This verse is very specific about Sarah HEARING the conversation)

11) Now Abraham and Sarah were old and well stricken in age; and it ceased to be with Sarah <u>after the manner of women</u>. (Sarah had stopped having her periods by then)

12) Therefore Sarah laughed within herself, saying, After I am waxed old (Abraham is 99 years old and Sarah is 89, well beyond her child bearing years in age) shall I have pleasure, my lord (Sarah was talking about Abraham being her lord) being old also?

13) And the LORD said unto Abraham, Wherefore did Sarah laugh, saying, Shall I of a surety bear a child, which am old?

14) Is any thing too hard for the LORD? <u>At the time appointed</u> I will return unto thee, according to the time of life, and <u>Sarah shall have a son</u>.

15) Then <u>Sarah denied, saying, I laughed not; for she was afraid</u>. And he said, <u>Nay; but thou didst laugh</u>. (Short and to the point again. Even with God right there, Sarah denies saying she doubts God)

16) And the men rose up from thence, and looked toward Sodom: and Abraham went with them to bring them on the way.

17) And the LORD said, Shall I hide from Abraham that thing which I do;

33) And the LORD went his way, as soon as he had left communing with Abraham: and Abraham returned unto his place. (Abraham and Sarah are still in Hebron, the plain of Mamre)

Genesis 19   If you want to read the whole story about Lot and Sodom and Gomorrah, Heavenly Angel Lay Lay told me about it, it's in my book MATTHEW'S WORD 'TWO':REAL WORD OF GOD BIBLE

Genesis 20:1-18
1) And Abraham journeyed from thence toward the south country, and <u>dwelled (lived) between Kadesh and Shur, and sojourned (stayed shortly) in Gerar</u> (Abraham moved from Hebron to between Kadesh and Shur and visited Gerar. Now remember, **the land between Kadesh and Shur is considered the south country**).

2) And Abraham said <u>of Sarah his wife</u>, She is my sister: and Abimelech king of Gerar sent, and took Sarah (Mentions Sarah again. This is the third recorded time Abraham and Sarah are not sleeping together. The first time is when Sarah was taken by Pharaoh the king of Egypt, the second time was when Abraham and Hagar were sleeping together, this is the third time Abraham and Sarah are not

sleeping together).

3) But God came to Abimelech in a dream by night, and said to him, Behold, thou art but a dead man, for the woman which thou hast taken; for she is a man's wife.

4) But **Abimelech had not come near her** (This is extremely important. There are some 'false religions' that think Abimelech made love to Sarah that night and that's how Sarah conceived Isaac. This scripture right here clearly states that no one, including Abimelech or anyone else for that matter had done anything with Sarah while Sarah was in the care of Abimelech. Sarah conceives Isaac from Abraham's sperm after Sarah is released by Abimelech): and he (Abimelech) said, LORD, wilt thou slay also a righteous nation?

5) Said he (Abraham) not unto me (Abimelech), She is my sister? and she (Sarah), even she herself said, He is my brother: in the integrity of my heart and innocency of my hands have I done this.

6) And God said unto him in a dream, Yea, I know that thou didst this in the integrity of thy heart; for I also withheld thee from sinning against me (People who sin against Christians are actually sinning against God, Himself): therefore suffered I thee not to touch her (God, Himself, says right here that **God made sure Sarah was not sexually known** by anyone in Abimelech's command or kingdom. Abraham was 99 and Sarah was 89).

7) Now therefore restore the man his wife; for he is a prophet, and he shall pray for thee, and thou shalt live: and if thou restore her not, know thou that thou shalt surely die, thou, and all that are thine. (God's warning to Abimelech, just like He warns us, but we don't listen until it's too late)

8) Therefore Abimelech rose early in the morning, and called all his servants, and told all these things in their ears: and the men were sore afraid.

9) Then Abimelech called Abraham, and said unto him, What hast thou done unto us? and what have I offended thee, that thou hast brought on me and on my kingdom a great sin? thou hast done deeds unto me that ought not to be done.

10) And Abimelech said unto Abraham, What sawest thou, that thou hast done this thing?

11) And Abraham said, Because I thought, Surely the fear of God is not in this place; and they will slay me for my wife's sake.

12) And yet indeed she is my sister; she is the daughter of my father, but not the daughter of my mother; and she became my wife. (This is still a lie, once a man and woman consummate a marriage, they become one flesh and are no longer two, but one. Sarah was no longer Abraham's sister, but one with him as his wife. That's the difference between the Spirit and the Flesh, in the flesh she will always be Abraham's half-sister, but God doesn't count the flesh, only the Spirit, and in the Spiritual World, Sarah is Abraham's wife. The Spiritual World always over-rules the Physical World)

13) And it came to pass, when God caused me (Abraham) to wander from my father's house, that I said unto her (Sarah), This is thy kindness which thou shalt shew unto me; at every place whither we shall come, say of me (Abraham), He (Abraham) is my brother. (Why would Abraham want Sarah to say that Sarah is Abraham's sister at every place they stop? Abraham knew God was with him. Not enough faith in God perhaps)

14) And Abimelech took sheep, and oxen, and menservants, and womenservants, and gave them unto Abraham, and restored him Sarah his wife.

15) And Abimelech said, Behold, my land is before thee: <u>dwell where it pleaseth thee</u>. (still in Gerar)

16) And unto Sarah he said, Behold, I have given <u>thy brother</u> a thousand pieces of silver: behold, he is to thee a covering of the eyes, unto all that are with thee, and with all other: thus she was reproved. (Why did Abimelech address Abraham as Sarah's sister? To keep the secret that Abraham and Sarah were married and that wasn't even meant to be a secret to begin with)

17) So Abraham prayed unto God: and <u>God healed Abimelech, and his **wife**</u>, and his maidservants; and they bare children. (This is interesting, in a land that is full of women servants and concubines, Abimelech has only ONE WIFE, that's better than Abraham, Abraham has two wives up to this point. Sarah and Hagar)

18) For <u>the LORD had fast closed up all the wombs of the house of Abimelech</u>, because of Sarah Abraham's wife. (This tells us <u>Abraham and Sarah were still in Gerar for at least a few months and probably a</u>

lot longer. None of the women weren't getting pregnant. As I said, this is the third time Abraham and Sarah were not sleeping together. Talk about doubting God, here Abraham actually saw God face to face and two Heavenly Male Angels with God and Abraham and Sarah still doubted. Heavenly Angel Lay Lay did say, 'even the prophets and apostles sinned', they were no better than humans are today. We don't have to put the prophets and apostles on a pedestal thinking God can't use us in those Supernatural Ways. Jesus, Himself, used me in several Supernatural Ways and when I first started out helping Rachel I had no idea how to deal with anything in the Supernatural World. Jesus took my hand and led me through all of it step by step)

Genesis 21:1-34

1 And the LORD **visited** Sarah as he had said, and the LORD did unto Sarah as he had spoken. (God just allowed Abraham, 99 to get Sarah pregnant, 89. Now remember, Abraham and Sarah are in Gerar along with Hagar and Ishmael. Now, I have heard some say that Sarah actually saw God, but this doesn't say that. Sarai was in the tent when Abram actually saw God and the two angels and this verse doesn't say Sarah saw God, it says 'the LORD **visited** Sarah as he had said'. There is a big difference. Sarah could have been asleep or God could have been invisible when He visited Sarah. There is no indication Sarah ever saw God)

2) For **Sarah conceived, and bare Abraham** a son in his old age, at the set time of which God had spoken to him. (Abraham is 100 and Sarah is 90 now)

3) And Abraham called the name of his son that was born unto him, whom Sarah bare to him, Isaac. (Isaac was born in Gerar)

4) And Abraham circumcised his son Isaac being eight days old, as God had commanded him.

5) And **Abraham was an hundred years old**, when his son Isaac was born unto him.

6) And Sarah said, God hath made me to laugh, so that all that hear will laugh with me.

7) And she said, Who would have said unto Abraham, that Sarah should have given children suck (breast fed)? for I have born him a

son in his old age.

8) And the child grew, and was weaned (No longer needed to be breast fed): and Abraham made a great feast the same day that Isaac was weaned. (there must have been a set time specified for children to be breast fed and weaned from their mother's breasts, how else could Abraham have known when to plan the day for a 'great feast'?)

9) And Sarah saw the son of Hagar the Egyptian, which she had born unto Abraham, mocking (Isaac is old enough for Ishmael to mock).

10) Wherefore she (Sarah) said unto Abraham, Cast out this bondwoman and her son for **the son of this bondwoman shall not be heir with my son** *even with* Isaac. (It was Sarai's idea to have Hagar bear the child for Abram's inheritance to begin with. Sarah defeated her own purpose, just like a lot of women today. The woman wants a Christian man and then the woman over-rules the Christian man. My question is, are women today being Christian Women in order to get a Christian Man or are they doing their 'own thing' and expecting a Christian Man to put up with them? Men weren't created to be equal to or under women or children, but over women and children, then after the fall, all authority went to man),

11) And the thing was very grievous in Abraham's sight because of his son (This is putting Abraham in a position of having to choose which of his two boys he wants to keep, that's not fair to him, or any other man. Both children are his even though Ishmael is not Sarah's. Even though God did not consider Ishmael, Abraham's son, Abraham still had feelings and love for Ishmael. Women, you shouldn't do this to your husbands, it's not fair to them. How would you like it if you had to choose which of your children you would never see again or choose which child you send certain death? Just like Satan World Order Headquarters made little six year old Rachael choose which person she would allow to die, either her father or her brother? This sounds like Step-parents and half-brothers and half-sisters, being forced to make a choice. It's not fair to anyone involved and makes the children feel not only unwanted, but also murderers, killers, possible physically through suicides, but for sure emotionally and psychologically. Children who feel unwanted find a way to get recognition even if it's committing crimes and eventually going to prison).

12) And God said unto Abraham, Let it not be grievous in thy sight because of the lad, and because of thy bondwoman (God knows how much that statement Sarah just said hurt Abraham so God stepped in); in all that Sarah hath said unto thee (you), hearken (listen) unto her voice (words) (Go ahead and do as Sarah requests); for in Isaac shall thy (your) seed (the child between Abraham and Sarah) be called. (Isaac is still the only son God considers Abraham's).

13) And so of the son of the bondwoman will I make a nation, **because he** *is* **thy seed** (God had to keep His promise to Abraham that Abraham's seed would be blessed, even though Ishmael was not God's intention, Ishmael still came from Abraham's sperm so God blessed Ishmael as well as Isaac, but in a different way. If the parent of a 'bastard' or a 'bitch' thinks their child is the same as a child born in wedlock, the child isn't. The children may be the same seed in one respect, the same sperm donor, but not the same egg donor or the egg donor, but not the same sperm donor, making the children different. Even the children born out of 'wedlock' from parents who live together, the children are not the same as the children born in 'wedlock'. There is no 'legal bond' between the father and mother who live together. Some parents don't even have an emotional bond with each other. God is actually talking about the difference between the 'Spiritual Bloodline', and the 'Proper Physical Bloodline', compared to the 'Physical Bloodline' that Heavenly Angel Lay Lay talked about. Ishmael is the 'Physical Bloodline' because of Abraham's sperm, but not the 'Proper Physical Bloodline' because Hagar is not in the 'Proper Physical Bloodline like Abraham is, even though Hagar may be in the same 'Spiritual Bloodline' now since she has been with Abraham and Sarah for so long, Hagar may have become a Christian by this time).

14) And Abraham rose up early in the morning, and took **bread**, and **a bottle** of water, and gave *it* unto Hagar, **putting** *it* **on her shoulder**, and the child, and sent her away: and she departed, and wandered in the wilderness of Beer-sheba (This is south of Gerar, she was heading back to Egypt where she was originally from. God didn't tell Abraham to give Hagar anything to take with her and Ishmael, not even the bread and water. Abraham did that out of the goodness of his heart. That's all that Hagar and Ishmael was allowed to take

though. No camels, no animals, <u>just a little bread and water for themselves</u>. **Only what Hagar could carry on her <u>one shoulder</u>**. (Now remember, Ishmael is big and old enough to carry something as well and Hagar had another shoulder she could have carried something on. Ishmael is at least fourteen years old now and possibly almost an adult. Abraham definitely had camels, he could have given Hagar a camel and Ishmael a camel and a few camels for food and water. When Abraham sends his servant to a land to search for a wife for Isaac, Abraham sends the servant with **ten camels** and goods as well. So we know Abraham definitely had goods and camels he could have sent with Hagar and Ishmael. Getting Isaac a wife happens in about 30 years later, but we need to remember that each time Abraham and Sarah were in Gerar the king gave them a lot of substances and when they separated from Lot to begin with, they separated because of all the substances between the two of them, so even at this time Abraham had a lot of wealth)

      Genesis 24:10

      10) And the servant took **ten camels** of the camels (This tells us, Abraham had well over just ten camels, the servant only took ten of the camels Abraham had) of his master, and departed; for all the goods of his master *were* in his hand: and he arose, and went to Mesopotamia, unto the city of Nahor. (What does this mean in modern terms when it comes to Hagar and Ishmael? Let's not forget that Hagar was considered Abraham's wife in the culture, they weren't just living together like a lot of couples do today. Hagar, Abraham's wife, received no alimony, no child support, no property settlements, no fifty percent of the net worth, no court battles where the only ones who really win are the attorneys and counselors. <u>Just what the woman can carry on her one shoulder</u>. Now Ishmael was over sixteen years old when all this took place. How do I know that? Lets go back to Genesis 18:23-27 for a minute)

      Genesis 18:23-27

      23) And Abraham took Ishmael his son, and all that were born in his house, and all that were bought with his money, every male among the men in Abraham's house; and circumcised the flesh of their foreskin in the selfsame day, as God had said unto him.

      24) And **Abraham *was* <u>ninety years old and nine</u>** (99

years old), when he was circumcised in the flesh of his foreskin.

25) **And Ishmael his son** *was* **thirteen years old, when he was circumcised in the flesh of his foreskin.**

26) **In the selfsame day was Abraham circumcised, and Ishmael his son** (Sarah wasn't even pregnant with Isaac yet).

27) And all the men of his house, born in the house, and bought with money of the stranger, were circumcised with him.

Genesis 20:1

1) And Abraham journeyed from thence toward the south country, and dwelled between Kadesh and Shur (lived in), and sojourned (had a short stay) in Gerar.

Genesis 21:4-8

4) **And Abraham circumcised his son Isaac being eight days old**, as God had commanded him.

5) And **Abraham was an hundred years old**, when his son **Isaac was born** unto him

(There is a year between the circumcision of Ishmael and birth of Isaac. Abraham could be pushing a hundred and one years old. Ishmael was circumcised at thirteen so Hagar was sent out of Abraham's house when Ishmael was at least fifteen and maybe more, because how can any infant be 'mocked'. Isaac had to be old enough to be 'mocked').

6) And Sarah said, God hath made me to laugh, *so that* all that hear will laugh with me (no one will believe it until it happens because both Abraham and Sarah are both too old in the physical sense).

7) And she said, Who would have said unto Abraham, that Sarah should have given children suck (this means that Sarah would breast feed and the only time a woman has milk in her breasts is when they have given birth to a child)? For I (Sarah) have born *him* (Abraham) a son (Isaac) in his (Abraham's) old age.

8) And the child (Isaac) grew, and was weaned (off Sarah's breast milk): and Abraham made a great feast the *same* day that Isaac was weaned (Now in order for Ishmael to be making fun of Isaac, Isaac must have been at the toddler stage in life, probably

getting into things like all children do. Isaac certainly was no infant and Ishmael was at least sixteen, well on his way to adulthood. We know for sure that Isaac was at least two years old, that was because Isaac was done sucking milk from Sarah and probably well into finger foods. That would make Abraham at least 102, Sarah at least 92, and Ishmael at least 16)

Genesis 21:1-34 continued

15) And the water was spent (Used up) in the bottle, and she (Hagar) cast (Put) the child (Ishmael) under one of the shrubs, (Now we know there was at least a little shade in the wilderness between Gerar and Egypt)

16) And she (Hagar) went, and sat her (Hagar) down over (A position directly above something, either resting on the top of something, or above the upper surface of something with a space in between) (Merriam-Webster) against (In the opposite direction of: in the opposite direction to the movement, angle, or position of something or somebody) (Merriam-Webster) (Hagar sat down with her back toward Ishmael) *him* (Ishmael) a good way off (in a distance), as it were a bowshot (The distance that an arrow travels when it has been shot from a bow): (Hagar left Ishmael under a shrub and left him there, moving from Ishmael the distance an arrow can be shot from a bow with her back towards him) for she (Hagar) said, Let me (Hagar) not see the death of the child (Ishmael) (Hagar was far enough away from Ishmael with her back toward him that Hagar would not be able to see or hear Ishmael die). And she (Hagar) sat over against *him* (With her back toward Ishmael), and lifted up her voice and wept (Hagar was crying and God didn't do anything).

17) And God heard **the voice of the lad** (Ishmael is crying to God as well. Just like Heavenly Angel Lay Lay said, 'The **children are going to be crying to God because of the abominations the parents have committed**. (The parents of the 'bastards' and 'bitches' will be powerless to help their own children); and the angel of God called to Hagar out of heaven, (Only after Ishmael started calling out to God) and said unto her, What aileth thee, Hagar? Fear not; for **God hath heard the voice of the lad** where he *is* [God didn't listen to Hagar, but to Ishmael, the child. Why did God hold Hagar guilty too?

Because Hagar allowed Abram to make love to her, she could have chosen death, but she chose to spread her legs for Abram instead. Hagar was accustomed to a servant's position allowing the lord (Abraham) to do as he chose with her. The customs of any land never over-rule the King James Version of the Word of God. Just like Linda allowed Pastor Lee to have sex with her because she was accustomed to allow a 'Priest' from the Satanist Village to do as they chose with the servants and Linda saw Pastor Lee as a 'Priest' and authority figure. That's in my book MATTHEW'S WORD 'TWO':REAL WORD OF GOD BIBLE. After ten years of Abram and Sarai trying to get Sarai pregnant, everyone in Abram's camp knew that the child being Abram's heir was to be between Abram and Sarai, not Abram and a bondswoman]

18) Arise, lift up the lad, and hold him in thine hand (Go back to Ishmael and hold him. Notice that **the angel of the LORD only says this AFTER Ishmael calls out to God**, just as Heavenly Angel Lay Lay said, that the children will have to cry out to God from their own hearts, before God will intervene. The parents will have no control over the children's well being. Once the children cry out to God, reading the KJV, He will hear them and bless them, but only after they do as they need to according to His will, then He will intervene and help them); for I will make him a great nation.

19) And God opened her (Hagar's) eyes, and she (Hagar) saw a well of water (**God supplies the need only after Ishmael cries out to God**. So many people want proof now days, He will give them their proof, but not in the way they expect it. He will give the proof through their suffering children. Then the parents will listen to what Jesus is saying, not just hearing the words, but taking those words to their own hearts as well); and she (Hagar) went, and filled the bottle with water, and gave the lad drink [Even with her physical eyes opened, she couldn't see the physical water from the well. The water (His Word) was there all the time, Hagar just couldn't see the water with her Physical Eyes or hear it with her Physical Ears].

20) And God was with the lad (The term 'lad' tells us Ishmael was in his late teens to early adulthood); and he grew, and dwelt in the wilderness, and became an archer (This wilderness must have had some wild animals).

21) **And he dwelt in the wilderness of Paran**: and his mother (Hagar) took him (Ishmael) a wife out of the land of Egypt (Even after all the years Hagar stayed with Abraham and Sarah, Hagar chose to find Ishmael an Egyptian wife. Just because someone goes to church all the time doesn't mean they are a Christian. Remember, God didn't listen to Hagar, but to Ishmael. Hagar chose a wife, from her home land, the 'Physical Bloodline' that Heavenly Angel Lay Lay talked about in MATTHEW'S WORD 'TWO':REAL WORD OF GOD BIBLE. Hagar chose a woman who worshipped false gods for Ishmael to marry. Worshipping false gods is how Ishmael became a 'wild man', meaning he was possessed by an 'unclean spirit'. Ishmael wasn't even in the same 'Proper Physical Bloodline' as Isaac. Abraham was the prophet, not Isaac or Ishmael. Another point I need to make here is that even though Isaac may have been in the 'Proper Physical Bloodline' because Abraham and Sarah were both the direct descendents of Noah. They were both from Ur, the land of their ancestors. Hagar on the other hand was not from the 'Proper Physical Bloodline', she was from Egypt, the land of 'idol worshippers'. It takes both parents from the 'Proper Physical Bloodline' for the child to be a direct descendent in the 'Proper Physical Bloodline'. Ishmael definitely was not in the 'Proper Physical Bloodline'. Since Ishmael was never in the 'Proper Physical Bloodline', then Islam and Muslim are both from 'False Prophets' and 'Religious Unclean Spirits' to begin with. God flat out said, 'Isaac will be the heir', not Ishmael. God didn't even consider Ishmael the first born son of Abraham. God even told Abraham to use Isaac, **Abraham's only son** as a sacrifice for a burnt offering proving that **God did not consider Ishmael Abraham's son**)

22) And it came to pass at that time, that Abimelech and Phichol the chief captain of his host spake unto Abraham, saying, God is with thee in all that thou doest:

23) Now therefore swear unto me here by God that thou wilt not deal falsely with me, nor with my son, nor with my son's son: but according to the kindness that I have done unto thee, thou shalt do unto me, and to the land wherein thou hast sojourned (Stayed for a short time).

24) And Abraham said, I will swear.

25) And Abraham reproved (balled out) Abimelech because of a well of water, which Abimelech's servants had violently taken away.

26) And Abimelech said, I wot not (don't know) who hath done this thing; neither didst thou tell me, neither yet heard I of it, but to day. (Abimelech didn't know anything about the servants taking the well away from Abraham until that very minute when Abraham told Abimelech)

27) And Abraham took sheep and oxen, and gave them unto Abimelech; and both of them made a covenant.

28) And Abraham set seven ewe lambs of the flock by themselves.

29) And Abimelech said unto Abraham, What mean these seven ewe lambs which thou hast set by themselves? (Abimelech is wondering why Abraham has set aside the seven ewe lambs. Abraham and Sarah are still in Gerar and Isaac is born in Gerar because Abimelech is still around them and that's where Abimelech rules)

30) And he said, For these seven ewe lambs shalt thou take of my hand, that they may be a witness unto me, that I have digged this well. (Abraham is telling Abimelech that Abimelech is a witness of the well that Abraham had dug there so no one can take that well away from Abraham)

31) Wherefore he called that place Beersheba; because there they sware both of them.(Sarah is not with Abraham, Sarah is still in Gerar)

32) Thus they (Abraham and Abimelech) made a covenant at Beersheba: then Abimelech rose up, and Phichol the chief captain of his host, **and they returned into the land of the Philistines**. (This proves they were not in the land of the Philistines and Sarah is still in Gerar in the land of the Philistines. In this story the only time you heard of a king is when they were traveling either into Egypt or the Philistines and the only city they lived in when they were even close to the Philistines was Gerar, except when the four kings and five kings were fighting against each other. Looking on the maps, It looks like Gerar is right on the border of two countries, each time they go to Gerar, the king of the Philistines shows up)

33) And Abraham planted a grove in Beersheba, and called there on the name of the LORD, the everlasting God. (Abraham is still in Beersheba. From Gerar to Beersheba is approximately 20 miles.

This may not seem like a long distance, but by camel traveling a maximum of 12 miles a day it's a two day journey)

34) And Abraham sojourned (temporarily stayed) in the Philistines' land many days. (Abraham is back in Gerar with Sarah)

Genesis 22:1-24

1) And it came to pass after these things, that God did tempt Abraham (God does tempt us), and said unto him, Abraham: and he said, Behold, here I am.

2) And he (God) said, Take now thy son, thine only son Isaac, whom thou lovest, and get thee into the land of Moriah; and offer him there for a burnt offering upon one of the mountains which I will tell thee of.

3) And Abraham rose up early in the morning, and saddled his ass, and took two of his young men with him, and Isaac his son, and clave the wood for the burnt offering, and rose up, and went unto the place of which God had told him. (Sarah did not go with Abraham this time either. This verse is very specific about who went with Abraham)

4) Then on the third day Abraham lifted up his eyes, and saw the place afar off.

5) And Abraham said unto his young men, Abide ye here with the ass; and I and the lad. (Lad means boy or young man. This tells us that Sarah is still alive. Later in scripture we will find out that Isaac was 37 years old when Sarah died. Isaac was no longer a 'lad' when he was 37 years old) will go yonder and worship, and come again to you.

6) And Abraham took the wood of the burnt offering, and laid it upon Isaac his son; and he took the fire in his hand, and a knife; and they went both of them together.

7) And Isaac spake unto Abraham his father, and said, My father: and he said, Here am I, my son. And he said, Behold the fire and the wood: but where is the lamb for a burnt offering?

8) And Abraham said, My son, God will provide himself a lamb for a burnt offering: so they went both of them together.

9) And they (Abraham and Isaac. Sarah isn't mentioned because Sarah didn't go this time, she is back in Gerar) came to the place which God had told him (Abraham) of; and Abraham built an altar there, and laid the wood in order, and bound Isaac his son, and laid

him (Isaac) on the altar upon the wood.

10) And Abraham stretched forth his (Abraham's) hand, and took the knife to slay his (Isaac's) son.

11) **And the angel of the LORD called unto him out of heaven,** and said, Abraham, Abraham: and he (Abraham) said, Here *am* I.

12) And he (The angel of the LORD) said, Lay not thine (your) hand upon the lad, neither do thou any thing unto him (Isaac): for now I know that thou (you) fearest God, seeing thou (you) hast not withheld thy (your) son, **thine only *son*** from me (the LORD) (here is the first time God, Himself says Isaac is Abraham's **ONLY SON**. God doesn't consider Ishmael Abraham's son even though Ishmael was conceived by Abraham's sperm and raised by Abraham for over fourteen years. **GOD DOES NOT CONSIDER A CHILD BORN OUT OF WEDLOCK (A BASTARD OR A BITCH) AND TAKEN AWAY FROM THE FATHER THE FATHER'S CHILD, AND THE FATHER IS NOT RESPONSIBLE TO SUPPLY ANYTHING FOR THAT CHILD'S GROWTH**).

13) And Abraham lifted up his eyes, and looked, and behold behind *him* (Abraham) a ram caught in a thicket by his horns: and Abraham went and took the ram, and offered him (the ram) up for a burnt offering in the stead of his son (Now, has anyone ever wondered why God chose to give Abraham a ram? The ram's head is one of the symbols used by Satanist's and they are the ones who sacrifice children. Only Satan sacrifices children. The ram also played a role in the offspring of the 'sons of God' making it past the 'great flood').

14) And Abraham called the name of that place Jehovah jireh: as it is said *to* this day, In the mount of the LORD it shall be seen.

15) **And the angel of the LORD called unto Abraham out of heaven the second time,**

16) And said, By myself have I sworn, saith the LORD, for because thou hast done this thing and hast not withheld thy son, **thine only *son* [here is the SECOND TIME, GOD MAKES IT CLEAR BY SAYING 'THINE ONLY SON': EVEN THOUGH ABRAHAM TOOK HAGAR TO BE HIS WIFE AT SARAH'S REQUEST, GOD DIDN'T ACKNOWLEDGE THE MARRIAGE. THE LAW OF THE LAND OR THE CULTURE OF THE LAND WILL NEVER OVER-RULE THE WORD OF THE LIVING**

GOD. EVEN THOUGH HAGAR AND ISHMAEL IS BEING FORCED OUT BY ABRAHAM, ABRAHAM IS NOT RESPONSIBLE FOR ISHAMEL OR HAGAR'S WELL BEING IN ANY WAY WHATSOEVER. <u>GOD DOES NOT CONSIDER A CHILD BORN OUT OF WEDLOCK (A 'BASTARD' OR A 'BITCH') THE FATHER'S CHILD AND THE FATHER IS NOT RESPONSIBILE TO SUPPLY ANYTHING FOR THAT CHILD'S GROWTH. WHILE THE CHILD IS UNDER THE FATHER'S ROOF AND THE FATHER IS ALLOWED TO TEACH AND RAISE THE CHILD, THE FATHER IS RESPONSIBLE FOR THE CHILD'S GROWTH AND MATURITY. REMEMBER, ISHMAEL WAS CIRCUMCISED RIGHT ALONG WITH ABRAHAM ON THE SAME DAY AND ABRAHAM TAUGHT ISHMAEL FOR THE FIRST FOURTEEN TO FIFTEEN YEARS OF ISHMAEL'S LIFE</u>]:

17) That in blessing I will bless thee (you), and in multiplying I will multiply thy (your) seed as the start of the heaven, and as the sand which *is* upon the sea shore; and thy (your) seed shall possess the gate of his enemies;

18) And in thy (your) seed shall all the nations of the earth be blessed; because thou (you) hast obeyed my voice.

19) So Abraham returned unto his young men, and <u>they rose up and went together to Beer-Sheba; and Abraham dwelt at Beer-Sheba.</u> (There is no indication whatsoever that Sarah is even around, she is still in Gerar. These are two times now that Sarah isn't mentioned when it comes to Abraham traveling. All the other times Sarah's name is mentioned when it came to Abraham traveling. Abraham and Isaac are together, just like Heavenly Angel Lay Lay said, 'the boys need to spend most of the time with their real fathers after they are of the age of five or six to the age of majority.' Ishmael was the 'bastard' child. Ishmael was never in God's plan to begin with. Ishmael came along due to the free-will of Abraham and Sarah, Sarah literally begging Abraham to take Hagar into the bedroom several times until Hagar conceived and Abraham following Sarah's influence and Hagar allowing Abraham to know her in that respect, but God went ahead and blessed Ishmael anyway because Abraham pleaded with God. The angel of Heaven came and told Abraham

TWICE that **ISAAC is Abraham's ONLY SON**. I wonder what kind of friction this incident had between Abraham and Sarah, Sarah didn't know anything about Abraham taking Isaac to offer him for a sacrifice. How would Sarah like that? After all those years of waiting to have a child, then having to give that child up as a sacrifice to God. Sarah wouldn't even been able to say her last 'I love you' to Isaac. I'm sure it caused friction between Abraham and Sarah when Sarah found out even though it shouldn't have, God did command Abraham to do it, but God also stopped the sacrifice before Abraham even raised his hand to complete the task as well. I put that last part in here because there was actually a woman who did use her child as a sacrifice thinking God told her to do the sacrifice and the voice she was listening to was actually from a 'Religious Unclean Spirit'. The woman wasn't reading the King James Version of the Word of God, but one of the 'false doctrine bibles' made by 'Religious Unclean Spirits' on the market today)

Galatians 4:22-31

22) For it is written, that **Abraham had two sons, the one by a bondmaid, the other by a free woman**. (This scripture seems to contradict the other scriptures above, right? Well, it really doesn't. This scripture is actually confirming the other scripture. God is talking about the 'Spiritual Bloodline' as well as the 'Proper Physical Bloodline' and Galatians is talking about the 'Physical Bloodline'. That is explained by Heavenly Angel Lay Lay in detail in my book MATTHEW'S WORD 'TWO':REAL WORD OF GOD BIBLE).

23) But **he** (Ishmael and all of his descendants) *who was* **of the bondwoman was born after the flesh**; but he (Isaac and all of his descendants) of the **free woman *was* by promise**. (Bondage is of the flesh, the 'Physical Bloodline' as Heavenly Angel Lay Lay explained in the book MATTHEW'S WORD 'TWO':REAL WORD OF GOD BIBLE. The 'Physical Bloodline' is Satan's territory)

24) Which things are an allegory (a symbolic representation) (Merriam-Webster): for these are the two covenants; the one from the mount Sinai, which gendereth to bondage, which is Agar.

25) For this Agar is mount Sinai in Arabia, and answered to Jerusalem which now is, and is in bondage with her children.

26) But Jerusalem which is above free, which is the mother of

us all.

27) For it is written, Rejoice, *thou* (you) barren that bearest not (without children); break forth and cry, thou that travailest not: for the desolate hath many more children than she which hath an husband.

28) Now we, brethren, as Isaac was, are the children of promise (The Spiritual Bloodline).

29) But as then he that was born after the flesh persecuted him *that was born* after the Spirit, even so *it is* now. (how Ishmael mocked Isaac. The Physical Bloodline is still mocking the Spiritual Bloodline, but Isaac won over Ishmael just like the Spiritual Bloodline always wins over the Physical Bloodline)

30) Nevertheless what saith the scripture? **Cast out the bondwoman and her son: for the son of the bondwoman** (Physical Bloodline) **shall not be heir with the son of the freewoman** (Proper Physical Bloodline).

31) So then, brethren, we are not children of the bondwoman (that which is of the 'flesh'), but of the free (that which is of the 'spirit'. The difference between the 'Spiritual Bloodline' and the 'Physical Bloodline').

Genesis 23:1-20

1) And **Sarah was an hundred and seven and twenty years old**: these were the years of the life of Sarah. (Sarah was 127 years old when she died. Isaac was 37 at the time. Isaac didn't marry Rebekah until he was 40 years old. Sarah never met Rebekah)

2) And <u>Sarah died in Kirjatharba; the same is Hebron</u> in the land of Canaan: **and Abraham came to mourn for Sarah**, and to weep for her. (Isaac, 37 years old, didn't go to Sarah's funeral because he was grief stricken. Ishmael, 50 years old, didn't go to Sarah's funeral because what Sarah made Abraham do to him and Hagar. Abraham was 137 years old when Sarah died. How did Sarah get from Gerar to Hebron and when? Isaac took her, he was 37. Why didn't Abraham take Sarah? Abraham and Sarah were having problems. It was because of Sarah that Abraham took Hagar to begin with and it was because of Sarah that Hagar and Ishmael were both kicked out and had to live in the Desert of Paran. Do you really think that went over

well with Abraham? There is no indication when this separation took place, but it did. Every time Abraham moved his tent, or what we would consider his home, it is recorded. The last times after Sarah made Abraham kick Hagar and Ishmael out, there is no recording of Abraham and Sarah moving together. The scriptures do say, 'Sarah died in Kiriatharba; the same is Hebron in the land of Canaan'. Sarah had to have moved there before she got to the point she was unable to travel. At this point, Isaac didn't know that Sarah even had a part of removing Hagar and Ishmael)

3) And Abraham stood up from before his dead, and spake unto the sons of Heth, saying,

4) I am a stranger and a sojourner (Stay as a temporary residence) (Merriam-Webster) with you: give me a possession of a buryingplace with you, that I may bury my dead out of my sight.

5) And the children of Heth answered Abraham, saying unto him,

6) Hear us, my lord: thou art a mighty prince among us: in the choice of our sepulchers (Burial in a vault: the act of putting a dead body in a grave or tomb) (Merriam-Webster) bury thy dead; none of us shall withhold from thee his sepulcher (burial in a vault: the act of putting a dead body in a grave or tomb) (Merriam-Webster), but that thou mayest bury thy dead.

7) And Abraham stood up, and bowed himself to the people of the land, even to the children of Heth.

8) And he communed with them, saying, If it be your mind that I should bury my dead out of my sight; hear me, and intreat for me to Ephron the son of Zohar,

9) That he may give me the cave of Machpelah, which he hath, which is in the end of his field; for as much money as it is worth he shall give it me for a possession of a buryingplace amongst you.

10) And Ephron dwelt among the children of Heth: and Ephron the Hittite answered Abraham in the audience of the children of Heth, even of all that went in at the gate of his city, saying,

11) Nay, my lord, hear me: the field give I thee, and the cave that is therein, I give it thee; in the presence of the sons of my people give I it thee: bury thy dead.

12) And Abraham bowed down himself before the people of the land.

13) And he spake unto Ephron in the audience of the people of the

land, saying, But if thou wilt give it, I pray thee, hear me: I will give thee money for the field; take it of me, and I will bury my dead there.

14) And Ephron answered Abraham, saying unto him,

15) My lord, hearken unto me: the land is worth four hundred shekels of silver; what is that betwixt (between) me and thee? bury therefore thy dead.

16) And Abraham hearkened unto Ephron; and Abraham weighed to Ephron the silver, which he had named in the audience of the sons of Heth, four hundred shekels of silver, current money with the merchant.

17) And the field of Ephron which was in Machpelah, which was before Mamre, the field, and the cave which was therein, and all the trees that were in the field, that were in all the borders round about, were made sure.

18) Unto Abraham for a possession in the presence of the children of Heth, before all that went in at the gate of his city.

19) And after this, Abraham buried Sarah his wife in the cave of the field of Machpelah before Mamre: the same is Hebron in the land of Canaan.

20) And the field, and the cave that is therein, were made sure unto Abraham for a possession of a burying place by the sons of Heth.

(CONTINUED IN:
HEAVENLY ANGEL LAY LAY
EXPLAINS
THE BIBLICAL GROUNDS FOR
MARRIAGE, SEPARATION,
AND DIVORCE)

ABORTED BABIES

BIBLIOGRAPHY

BIBLIOGRAPHY

1. Merriam Webster's Collegiate Dictionary Tenth Edition (1993), United States of America.

2. The Holy Bible King James Version (1998), B. B. Kirkbride Bible Co., Inc. Indianapolis, IN..USA